CONTENT

BACON MAC 'N' CHEESE
1 - 2

CHEESY BOLOGNESE
3 - 4

TRADITIONAL HOT APPLE PIE
5 - 6

HASSELBACK sweet potatoes
7 - 8

ROAST SWEET POTATO MEDLEY
9 - 10

SWEET POTATO PASTA BAKE WITH
11 - 12

RICOTTA CANNELLONI bolognese bake
13 - 14

TUNA, TOMATO AND MOZZARELLA fusilli bake
15 - 16

CREAMY SWEET POTATO cauliflower bake
17 - 18

SPAGHETTI WITH CRISPY PANCETTA with four cheese ricotta
19 - 20

CHICKEN BIRYANI WITH CREAMY CORIANDER and mint sauce
21 - 22

MINCE AND chickpea curry
23 - 24

SPICY VINDALOO beef ribs
25 - 26

ONE-PAN BUTTER CHICKEN with cauliflower
27 - 28

CHOCOLATE pear loaf
29 - 30

PEAR AND ALMOND mug cake
31 - 32

MINI SPONGE CAKES WITH PEARS AND salted caramel sauce
33-34

BUTTERMILK & VANILLA BEAN scones
35 - 36

WAFFLES WITH CARAMEL, ICE CREAM and pears
37 - 38

Mushroom BREAKFAST TARTS
39 - 40

ZUCCHINI FRITTERS WITH PORTABELLA & POACHED EGG
41 - 42
WAFFLES WITH SAUTEED & MAPLE BACON
43 - 44
LAMB & FETA GOZLEME
45 - 46
MEDITERRANEAN & CHORIZO SKEWERS
47 - 48
THE "ULTIMATE" BEEF & BURGER
49 - 50
PORTABELLA Mushroom FRIES
51 - 52
Mushroom & LEEK FILO PIE
53 - 54
Mushroom VEGGIE BURGERS
55 - 56
Mushroom & CHAR SIU PORK STIR FRY
57 - 58
MAPLE ROASTED Mushroom & CARROT SALAD
59 - 60
SWEET POTATO and lentil patties
61 - 62
SWEET POTATO spinach and feta muffins
63 - 64
SWEET POTATO toast toppers
65 - 66
SWEET POTATO and broccoli frittata
67 - 68
MUSHROOM AND ancient grain salad
69 - 70
CAESAR SALAD with hot smoked salmon
71 - 72
TUNA AND PESTO pasta salad
73 - 74
LEMON AND HERB mushroom salad
75 - 76
GREEN shakshuka
77 - 78
ZOODLE AND mushroom salad
79 - 80

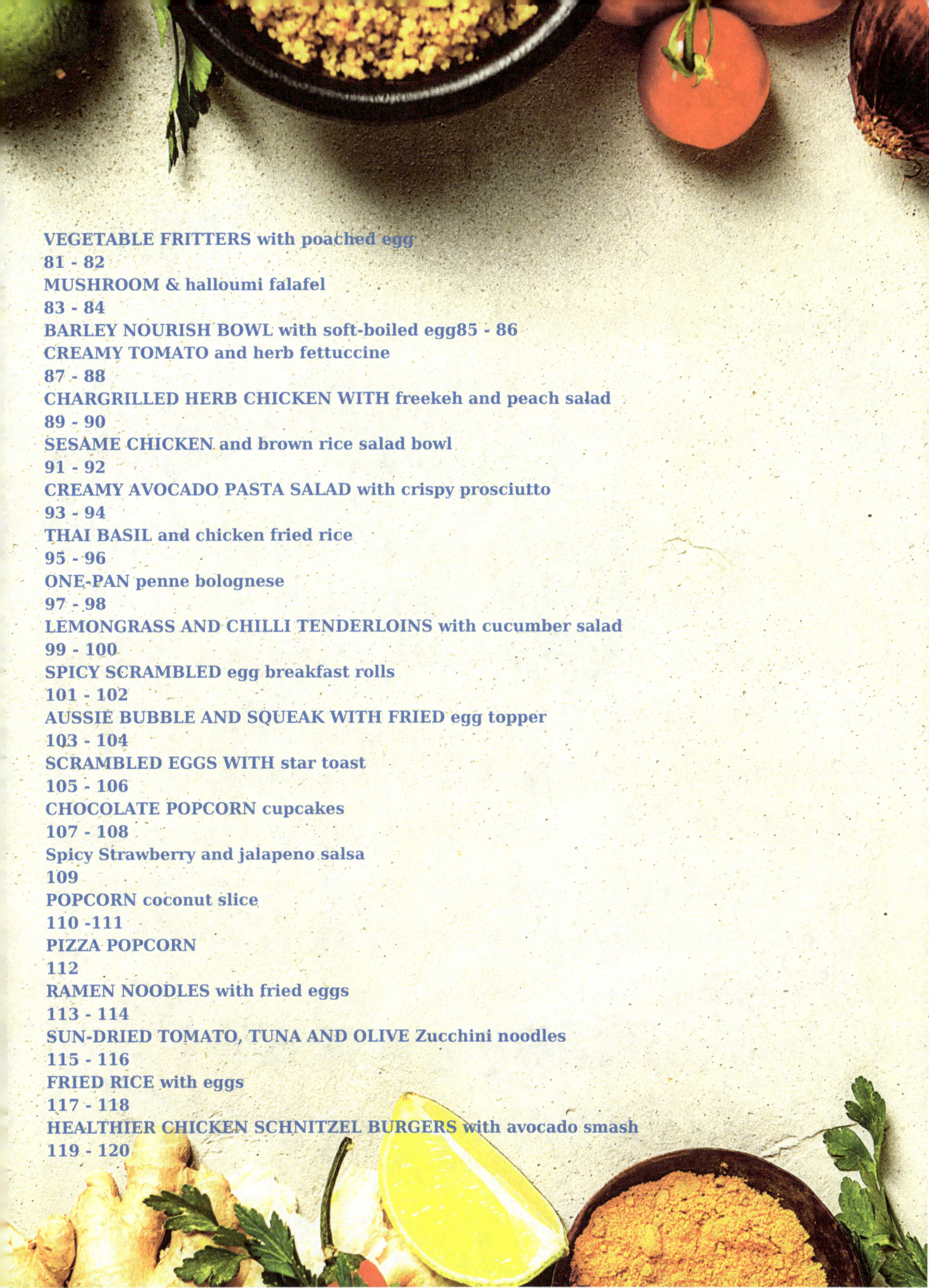

VEGETABLE FRITTERS with poached egg
81 - 82
MUSHROOM & halloumi falafel
83 - 84
BARLEY NOURISH BOWL with soft-boiled egg 85 - 86
CREAMY TOMATO and herb fettuccine
87 - 88
CHARGRILLED HERB CHICKEN WITH freekeh and peach salad
89 - 90
SESAME CHICKEN and brown rice salad bowl
91 - 92
CREAMY AVOCADO PASTA SALAD with crispy prosciutto
93 - 94
THAI BASIL and chicken fried rice
95 - 96
ONE-PAN penne bolognese
97 - 98
LEMONGRASS AND CHILLI TENDERLOINS with cucumber salad
99 - 100
SPICY SCRAMBLED egg breakfast rolls
101 - 102
AUSSIE BUBBLE AND SQUEAK WITH FRIED egg topper
103 - 104
SCRAMBLED EGGS WITH star toast
105 - 106
CHOCOLATE POPCORN cupcakes
107 - 108
Spicy Strawberry and jalapeno salsa
109
POPCORN coconut slice
110 -111
PIZZA POPCORN
112
RAMEN NOODLES with fried eggs
113 - 114
SUN-DRIED TOMATO, TUNA AND OLIVE Zucchini noodles
115 - 116
FRIED RICE with eggs
117 - 118
HEALTHIER CHICKEN SCHNITZEL BURGERS with avocado smash
119 - 120

Tip
You can make these jaffles with any leftover pasta dish

BACON MAC 'N' CHEESE *jaffles*

 PREP 10 MINS   **COOK** 6-8 MINS   **SERVES** 4

INGREDIENTS

1 cup (320 g) leftover Bacon Mac 'N' Cheese

8 slices thick-cut white or wholemeal bread

4 tablespoons (80 g) Western Star Spreadable Original Soft

4 Bega Tasty Farmers' or Country Light Natural Cheese Slices

METHOD

1. Preheat a jaffle maker. Warm Mac 'N' Cheese slightly in your microwave

2. Spread bread on both sides with Western Star Spreadable Original Soft

3. Dividing mixture evenly, top 4 slices of bread with the Mac 'N' Cheese, spreading out leaving a 1 cm border. Top each sandwich with a Bega Tasty Farmers' Natural Cheese Slice and then top with the remaining bread

4. Cooking in 2 batches, place Mac 'N' Cheese filled bread into the jaffle maker and cook for 3-4 minutes until golden and toasted. Serve with a leafy green salad, if liked

CHEESY BOLOGNESE *jaffles*

 **PREP** 10 MINS  **COOK** 6-8 MINS **SERVES** 4

INGREDIENTS

1⅓ cups (330 g) leftover Bolognese sauce

8 slices thick-cut white or wholemeal bread

4 tablespoons (80 g) Western Star Spreadable Original Soft

8 Bega Tasty Farmers' or Country Light Natural Cheese Slices

METHOD

1. Preheat a jaffle maker. Warm leftover Bolognese sauce slightly in your microwave

2. Spread each piece of bread on both sides with Western Star Spreadable Original Soft

3. Dividing mixture evenly, top 4 slices of bread with the Bolognese sauce, spreading out leaving a 1 cm border. Top each sandwich with 2 Bega Tasty Farmers' Natural Cheese Slices, and then top with the remaining bread

4. Cooking in 2 batches, place Bolognese-filled bread into the jaffle maker and cook for 3-4 minutes until golden and toasted. Serve with a side salad, if liked

TRADITIONAL HOT APPLE PIE
jaffles

PREP 12 MINS **COOK** 6-8 MINS **SERVES** 4

INGREDIENTS

300 mL Western Star Thickened Cream

2 cups canned pie fruit sliced apples

¼ cup sultanas

½ teaspoon ground cinnamon

Good pinch allspice

8 slices thick-cut white or wholemeal bread

4 tablespoons (80 g) Western Star Spreadable Original Soft

Icing sugar, for dusting

Maple syrup, for drizzling

METHOD

1. Using an electric hand mixer, whip Western Star Thickened Cream in a bowl until soft peaks form. Set aside
2. Preheat a jaffle maker. Combine apples, sultanas, cinnamon and allspice in a bowl
3. Spread bread on both sides with Western Star Spreadable Original Soft
4. Dividing mixture evenly, top 4 slices of bread with the apple mixture, spreading out leaving a 1 cm border. Top with the remaining bread
5. Cooking in 2 batches, place apple-filled bread into the jaffle maker and cook for 3-4 minutes until golden and toasted
6. Dust with icing sugar and serve with whipped cream and a drizzle of maple syrup. Scatter with fresh strawberries, if liked

HASSELBACK
sweet potatoes

 PREP 15 MINS   **COOK** 1 HOUR 10 MINS   **MAKES** 6

INGREDIENTS

6 x 200g Sweet Potatoes, scrubbed

6 sprigs fresh thyme, plus extra for serving

Olive oil

¼ teaspoon sea salt

⅓ cup finely grated parmesan

METHOD

1. Preheat oven to 200°C/180°C. Carefully cut 3mm slices into the sweet potatoes, leaving 5mm intact at the bottom. Place on a baking-paper lined oven tray
2. Strip the leaves from the thyme and tuck in between the fans of the sweet potatoes
3. Drizzle with oil and sprinkle with salt
4. Bake for 1 hour -1 hour 10 minutes until golden and soft in the middle when easily pierced with a knife. Serve sprinkled with parmesan

Tip: The perfect side for a hearty roast chicken or beef.

ROAST SWEET POTATO MEDLEY
with rib-eye steak

 PREP 10 MINS   **COOK** 50 MINS   **SERVES** 4

INGREDIENTS

400g each Gold, Purple and White Sweet Potato, chopped

3 tablespoons olive oil, plus extra for steaks

½ bunch fresh thyme sprigs

4 x beef rib-eye steaks

Mustard, to serve

METHOD

1. Preheat oven to 200°C/180°C. Line two oven trays with baking paper. Combine sweet potatoes evenly on trays. Toss with olive oil to coat and season. Bake for 35-40 minutes until golden and tender

2. Meanwhile, drizzle steaks with extra oil. Sprinkle both sides with salt and pepper. Cook steaks in a large oven-proof frying pan over medium-high heat for 2-3 minutes each side until browned. Transfer pan to oven and cook for about 5 minutes until cooked to taste. Rest steaks for 5 minutes

3. Serve steaks with potato medley and mustard

TIP: Twist it by serving the rib-eye steaks with hasselback sweet potatoes for dinner party wow or with sweet potato mash for when time is of the essence.

SWEET POTATO PASTA BAKE WITH
spinach and pine nuts

 **PREP** 20 MINS  **COOK** 50 MINS  **SERVES** 6

INGREDIENTS

350g penne or other pasta

1 tablespoon olive oil

1 small onion, finely chopped

2 garlic cloves, crushed

500g lean beef mince

400g Sweet Potato, peeled, coarsely grated

1 small zucchini, coarsely grated

2 tablespoons tomato paste

400g can diced tomatoes

1 cup salt-reduced beef stock

4 sprigs thyme

50g baby spinach leaves

100g ricotta

½ cup (40g) grated parmesan

2 tablespoons pine nuts

METHOD

1. Cook pasta in a large pan of salted, boiling water until al dente. Drain well

2. Meanwhile, heat oil in a medium pan on medium-high heat. Cook onion and garlic for 3-4 minutes until softened. Add beef and cook until browned, breaking up lumps with a spoon. Add sweet potato and zucchini. Cook for 2 minutes until softened slightly

3. Add paste, tomatoes, stock and thyme. Simmer, uncovered for 15-20 minutes until thickened slightly. Stir through spinach leaves until wilted

4. Meanwhile, preheat oven to 220°C/200°C fan-forced

5. Combine pasta and beef mixture in an 8-cup capacity ovenproof dish. Sprinkle with ricotta, parmesan and pine nuts. Bake for 15-20 minutes until golden

RICOTTA CANNELLONI
bolognese bake

PREP 10 MINS   **COOK** 1 HOUR 20 MINS   **SERVES** 4

INGREDIENTS

2 tbsp olive oil

500g quality minced beef

1 brown onion, finely chopped

2 garlic cloves, finely chopped

1 carrot, peeled and finely chopped

2 celery sticks, finely chopped

2 x tins whole peeled tomatoes

200ml red wine (or water)

1 x 500g tub Perfect Italiano Ricotta

Zest of 1 lemon

200g cannelloni

150g Perfect Italiano Grated Perfect Bakes Cheese

METHOD

1. Heat the oil in a large pan over a medium heat. Once hot, add the mince and use a wooden spoon to break up. Continue to stir and cook for 5 minutes or until the mince has browned. Add the onion, garlic, carrot and celery and continue to cook for 10 minutes or until the vegetables have softened. Add the tomatoes and wine (or water) and stir, breaking up tomatoes with the back of the wooden spoon. Bring the mixture to a simmer and then reduce the heat to low. Simmer for 30 minutes, stirring regularly. Season to taste and set aside to cool slightly

2. Preheat the oven to 180°C

3. To prepare the cannelloni, mix the Perfect Italiano Ricotta with the lemon zest, and then season with salt and pepper. Carefully fill the cannelloni with the ricotta using a knife or piping bag

4. Spoon half of the Bolognese into a large baking dish and then gently lay the filled cannelloni into the dish. Top the cannelloni with the remaining Bolognese and then sprinkle over the Perfect Italiano Perfect Bakes Cheese. Place the dish into the oven and bake for 35 minutes or until golden and bubbling

5. Remove from the oven, and allow to sit for 5 minutes before serving

Recipe by **Perfect Italiano** | perfectitaliano.com.au

tip

For something a bit more fancy, replace tuna with flaked salmon

TUNA, TOMATO AND MOZZARELLA
fusilli bake

 **PREP** 5 MINS    **COOK** 35 MINS   **SERVES** 4

INGREDIENTS

400g fusilli

1 tbsp olive oil

2 garlic cloves, sliced

400g tomato passata

425g chopped tomatoes

10 basil leaves, torn

⅓ cup pitted kalamata olives, chopped

1 x 425g tin tuna in spring water, drained and flaked

200g Perfect Italiano Mozzarella Cheese

METHOD

1. Cook the fusilli according to packet instructions, drain and set aside
2. Preheat the oven to 180°C
3. Heat the olive oil in a large deep-sided pan over a medium heat. Add the garlic and fry for 1 minute before adding the passata and chopped tomatoes. Bring to a simmer and then reduce the heat to low. Add the basil and olives and mix well. Continue to simmer for 5 minutes and then season with salt and pepper to taste
4. Add the drained pasta and tuna to the sauce, and mix well to coat the pasta and break up tuna. Transfer the mixture to a baking dish and sprinkle over the Perfect Italiano Mozzarella. Carefully place in the oven to bake for 20-25 minutes or until golden brown
5. Remove from the oven and allow to sit for 5 minutes before serving

Tip
Serve as a side dish to meat or fish or as a main with a fresh green salad.

CREAMY SWEET POTATO
cauliflower bake

PREP 10 MINS   **COOK** 1 HOUR   **SERVES** 4

INGREDIENTS

400g sweet potato, peeled and sliced into 1cm slices

¼ head cauliflower, cut into 2cm slices

200ml cream

200ml milk

2 garlic cloves, peeled

⅓ cup Perfect Italiano Grated Parmesan

4 sprigs thyme, leaves removed

250g Perfect Italiano Perfect Bakes

METHOD

1. Preheat the oven to 180°C
2. Arrange the sweet potato and cauliflower into the dish so that the vegetables fit snuggly
3. Combine the cream, milk and garlic in a small saucepan and place over a low heat. Bring to a simmer and then turn off the heat. Stir through the Perfect Italiano Parmesan and the thyme, and then season with salt and pepper. Set aside for a couple of minutes before removing the garlic cloves
4. Carefully pour the cream mixture over the vegetables and then cover the baking dish with foil. Place into the oven to bake for 30 minutes
5. Remove from the oven and sprinkle over the Perfect Italiano Perfect Bakes. Return to the oven uncovered for a further 30 minutes or until golden. The vegetables should be tender when pierced with a knife
6. Remove from the oven and serve

tip

Pancetta can be substituted with streaky bacon if not available

SPAGHETTI WITH CRISPY PANCETTA
with four cheese ricotta

PREP 5 MINS **COOK** 10 MINS **SERVES** 4

INGREDIENTS

500g spaghetti

1 tbsp olive oil

4 slices pancetta, chopped

450g Ricotta Pasta Stir Through, Four Cheese

Salt and Pepper to taste

⅓ cup chives, finely chopped, to garnish

Perfect Italiano Shaved Parmesan, to serve

METHOD

1. Cook pasta according to packet instructions
2. Meanwhile, add olive oil to a large pan and place over medium to high heat. Once hot add the pancetta and fry until crispy and golden. Turn heat to low and add drained cooked pasta to the pan
3. Add Ricotta Pasta Stir Through, Four Cheese to the pot and gently stir through
4. Once warmed through, season to taste and garnish with chives and Perfect Italiano Shaved Parmesan

CHICKEN BIRYANI WITH CREAMY CORIANDER
and mint sauce

 PREP 10 MINS **COOK** 55 MINS **SERVES** 4

INGREDIENTS

1 cup thick plain yoghurt

½ cup mint leaves, roughly chopped

½ cup coriander leaves, roughly chopped

1 lemon, juiced

2 cups basmati rice

1 tablespoon vegetable oil

1 brown onion, diced

500g chicken thigh fillets, diced

375g Passage to India Biryani simmer sauce

⅓ cup sultanas

Toasted natural flaked almonds, to serve

Coriander sprigs, to serve

METHOD

1. Place yoghurt, mint leaves and coriander leaves into a small food processor and pulse until a smooth pale green sauce forms. Transfer to a bowl. Stir through ¼ cup lemon juice, salt and white pepper

2. Rinse rice until water runs clear. Place into a medium saucepan and cover with water. Place over a high heat and bring to the boil. Reduce heat to low, cover and cook for 8 minutes. Drain

3. Heat oil in a frying pan over a medium high heat. Add onion and chicken and cook for 8 minutes or until browned. Pour Passage to India Biryani simmer sauce over chicken and bring to the boil. Reduce heat to low and simmer for 10 minutes

4. Sprinkle sultanas over chicken mixture. Spoon rice evenly over chicken and sultanas. Cover with a sheet of baking paper, tucking into side of pan. Cover and cook for 10 minutes. Remove from heat and stand for 10 minutes. Sprinkle with toasted almonds. Serve with coriander & mint sauce and coriander sprigs

Tip
Served with steamed rice, if preferred.

MINCE AND
chickpea curry

 PREP 15 MINS   **COOK** 25 MINS   **SERVES** 4

INGREDIENTS

1 tablespoon vegetable oil

1 brown onion, diced

500g beef mince

375g Passage to India Mild Mince Curry simmer sauce

400g can chickpeas, drained, rinsed

3 tomatoes, seeds removed, finely diced

1 Lebanese cucumber, seeds removed, finely diced

1 small red onion, finely diced

1 lemon, finely grated rind and ¼ cup juice

¼ cup finely chopped mint

Naan or Roti bread, warmed, to serve

Thick plain yoghurt, to serve

Mint sprigs, to serve

METHOD

1. Heat oil in a deep frying pan over medium heat. Add onion and cook for 5 minutes or until softened. Add mince and stir with a wooden spoon to break up mince. Cook for 8 minutes or until browned. Pour Passage to India Mild Mince Curry simmer sauce over mince and stir until well combined. Bring to the boil, reduce heat to low and cook for 15 minutes or until slightly thickened. Stir through chickpeas. Cook for 2 minutes or until heated through. Season with salt and pepper

2. Meanwhile, combine tomato, cucumber, red onion, lemon rind, lemon juice and mint in a bowl. Prepare bread as per packet instructions

3. Place a naan or roti bread onto each serving plate. Top with curried mince, tomato & mint sambal, a dollop of yoghurt and mint sprigs. Serve immediately

SPICY VINDALOO
beef ribs

 PREP 10 MINS   **COOK** 1.5 HOURS   **SERVES** 4

INGREDIENTS

1.2kg beef ribs

2 tablespoons vegetable oil

2 small red onion, cut into thin wedges

375g Passage to India Vindaloo simmer sauce

2 teaspoons mustard seeds

1 teaspoon cumin seeds

3 carrots, shredded

⅓ cup coriander leaves, plus extra to serve

Steamed basmati rice, to serve

Finely sliced red chilli, to serve (optional)

METHOD

1. Place ribs into a saucepan and cover with cold water. Place over a high heat and bring to the boil. Reduce heat and simmer for 25 minutes. Remove from heat and cool in liquid. Drain. Cut ribs into smaller pieces

2. Heat half the oil in a deep frying pan over medium heat. Add half the onion and cook for 3 minutes or until softened. Add Passage to India Vindaloo simmer sauce and bring to the boil. Add beef ribs and stir until coated with sauce. Reduce heat to low, cover and simmer for 1 hour or until beef is tender

3. Meanwhile, heat remaining oil in a frying pan over medium heat. Add remaining onion and cook for 3 minutes or until softened. Add mustard seeds and cumin seeds. Cook for 2 minutes or until aromatic. Add carrots and cook for 3 minutes or until just softened. Remove from heat and season with salt and white pepper. Stir through coriander leaves just before serving. Spoon rice onto serving plates. Top with ribs and sauce and serve with carrot salad, extra coriander and chilli, if you like

ONE-PAN BUTTER CHICKEN
with cauliflower

PREP 5 MINS   **COOK** 35 MINS   **SERVES** 4

INGREDIENTS

1 tablespoon vegetable oil

8 chicken thigh cutlets, with skin on

1 brown onion, thinly sliced

½ (500g) cauliflower, cut into florets

375g Passage to India Butter Chicken Simmer Sauce

Steamed basmati rice, to serve

Roasted salted cashews, roughly chopped, to serve

Coriander sprigs, to serve

METHOD

1. Heat oil in a large non-stick frying pan over medium heat. Add chicken pieces and cook for 10 minutes or until browned on all sides. Transfer to a plate. Drain excess fat and discard

2. Add onion and cauliflower to pan and cook for 5 minutes or until softened. Pour Passage to India Butter Chicken Simmer Sauce over vegetables and bring to a simmer. Return chicken pieces to pan, coating well with sauce. Cover pan, reduce heat and simmer for 20 minutes or until chicken is cooked through.

3. Spoon rice onto a platter. Top with chicken, vegetables and sauce. Sprinkle with cashew nuts and coriander

CHOCOLATE
pear loaf

 **PREP** 15 MINS   **COOK** 1 HOUR   **MAKES** 1

INGREDIENTS

540g Devil's Food cake mix

3 eggs

¾ cup water

⅓ cup vegetable oil

4 medium pears, core removed from base

2 tablespoons icing sugar

METHOD

1. Preheat oven to 180°C. Grease and line a 27cm x 11.5cm x 6.5cm deep (base measurement) (8 cup capacity) loaf pan with baking paper. Prepare cake mix as per packet instructions. Spoon one-third of cake batter into the base of prepared loaf pan. Stand pears in cake batter. Spoon remaining cake batter around and over pears until covered

2. Bake loaf for 50-60 minutes or until cooked through when tested in the centre with a skewer. Allow to stand for 10 minutes before transferring loaf to a wire rack to cool. Dust with icing sugar and serve

Tip: We used Betty Crocker Devil's Food Cake mix.

Tip

If you don't have a microwave, bake in the oven for 10 min at 180°C

PEAR AND ALMOND
mug cake

 **PREP** 10 MINS  **COOK** 1 MIN   **SERVES** 4

INGREDIENTS

1 large pear
⅔ cup self-raising flour
2 tablespoons almond meal
2 tablespoons caster sugar
2 eggs
⅓ cup milk
40g butter, melted and cooled
½ teaspoon vanilla
¼ cup maple syrup, to serve
Icing sugar, to dust

METHOD

1. Finely dice half the pear and cut remaining half into thin wedges. Combine flour, almond meal and sugar in a small bowl. Whisk egg, milk, butter and vanilla in a jug. Add to flour mixture and stir until combined. Stir through diced pear

2. Spoon cake batter into 4 x ¾ cup capacity cups. Microwave on high for 60-70 seconds or until cake has risen and top is just set. Stand pear wedges up in cooked cakes. Drizzle with maple syrup and dust with icing sugar. Serve immediately

MINI SPONGE CAKES WITH PEARS AND *salted caramel sauce*

 **PREP** 10 MINS   **SERVES** 6

INGREDIENTS

225g unfilled rectangular sponge slab

150ml tub double thick cream

2 small pears, quartered, core removed, cut into thin wedges

⅓ cup purchased salted caramel flavoured topping

50g hokey pokey honeycomb bar, finely chopped

METHOD

1. Cut sponge slab into 6 squares or using a biscuit cutter, cut into 7cm rounds. Place sponge cake onto serving plates. Top with cream and pear wedges. Drizzle over caramel topping and sprinkle with hokey pokey. Serve

Tip

A pear-fect dessert ready in 10 minutes

BUTTERMILK & VANILLA BEAN
scones

 PREP 20 MINS   **COOK** 20-23 MINS   **MAKES** 12

INGREDIENTS

3 cups self-raising flour

2 teaspoons baking powder

½ teaspoon salt

¼ cup caster sugar

4 tablespoons (80 g) Western Star Spreadable Original Soft, chilled

1½ cups buttermilk (plus extra for brushing)

1 teaspoon vanilla bean paste or extract

Icing sugar, for dusting

300 mL Western Star Thickened Cream, whipped, and raspberry jam, to serve

METHOD

1. Preheat oven to 220°C/200°C fan-forced. Place flour, baking powder, salt and sugar into a large bowl. Dot with the Western Star Spreadable Original Soft. Using your fingertips, rub together until mixture resembles fine breadcrumbs

2. Make a well in the centre of the dry ingredients. Whisk buttermilk and vanilla in a jug. Pour mixture into dry ingredients. Using a dinner knife, quickly mix until just combined (add a little more buttermilk to the mixture if needed). Pull dough together into a rough ball. Turn onto a lightly floured surface and gently knead just until a smooth dough forms. Press the dough into a 3 cm thick circle. Using a 5 cm cookie cutter dusted with flour, cut 12 rounds from the dough (re-rolling dough as necessary)

3. Place scones close together onto a lightly greased baking tray lined with baking paper. Brush tops with extra buttermilk. Bake for 20-23 minutes until pale golden and cooked through. Remove scones from pan and wrap in a clean tea-towel. Set aside to cool slightly

4. Dust warm scones with icing sugar. Serve split scones topped with whipped cream and raspberry jam. Add fresh seasonal berries, if liked

Tip
These pears can be served on top of pancakes as well.

WAFFLES WITH CARAMEL ICE CREAM
and pears

 **PREP** 5 MINS **COOK** 10 MINS **SERVES** 6

INGREDIENTS

25g butter

2 tablespoon brown sugar

6 small pears, peeled, halved

6 thick waffles

Salted caramel ice cream, to serve

METHOD

1. Melt butter in a frying pan over medium heat. When sizzling add the brown sugar and stir until sugar has melted. Add pears, cut side down and cook for 3 minutes. Turn and cook for 3 minutes or until pears are caramelised and softened. Remove from heat and cool

2. Toast waffles and place onto serving plates. Top with a small scoop of ice cream. Place pear and sauce over ice cream and serve immediately

Much **BETTER BREAKFAST**

Mushroom BREAKFAST TARTS

Prep: 10 mins   Cook: 15 mins   Serves: 6

Ingredients

- 2 tbsp olive oil
- 200g Button Mushrooms, trimmed and quartered
- 4 (100g) bacon rashers, trimmed and chopped (1cm pieces)
- 1 red capsicum, finely chopped
- 2 tbsp chopped thyme leaves, plus sprigs to garnish
- 3 sheets puff pastry
- 6 eggs

Method

1. Heat oil in a large frying pan over medium high heat. Cook mushrooms for 4-5 minutes or until golden. Add bacon and thyme and cook for 2-3 minutes or until bacon is crisp. Add capsicum, cook for 2 minutes

2. Preheat oven to 200°C fan forced. Lightly grease 6 x 10.5cm (base) loose base fluted tart tins. Using a 14cm cutter, cut 6 rounds from the pastry. Line pans with pastry, prick well with a fork and trim the edges

3. Place tins on a baking tray and cook for 15 minutes or until pastry is just golden. When cool enough to touch, gently push pastry down into the base

4. Break an egg into each pastry shell, top with mushroom mixture. Cook in oven for 10-12 minutes or until egg white is cooked and yolk is slightly runny. Serve with thyme sprigs to garnish

Much **BETTER BREAKFAST**

ZUCCHINI FRITTERS WITH PORTABELLA *Mushrooms* & POACHED EGG

Prep: 10 mins   Cook: 15 mins   Serves: 4   Makes: 8 Fritters

Ingredients

- 4 (240g) Portabella Mushrooms, thickly sliced
- 50g butter
- 240g truss cherry tomatoes, cut into 4 lengths
- ¾ cup olive oil
- 350g zucchini, grated
- 100g halloumi cheese, chopped
- 1 tsp sweet paprika
- 2 green onions, thinly sliced
- 6 eggs
- ½ cup (75g) self raising flour
- ⅓ cup (75ml) milk

Method

1. Heat butter in a large saucepan over medium heat. Once melted, add mushrooms and cook for 5 minutes or until tender and lightly browned. Remove mushrooms and set aside
2. Meanwhile, preheat oven to 180°C fan forced. Line a baking tray with baking paper. Place cherry tomatoes on the baking tray and drizzle with 2 tablespoons olive oil. Season with salt and pepper. Cook for 10-12 minutes or until tomatoes have softened
3. Using hands squeeze zucchini to remove any excess liquid. Combine zucchini, halloumi, paprika and green onion in a medium bowl. Season with salt and pepper. Combine flour, 2 eggs and milk in a separate bowl. Add zucchini mixture and stir gently until combined
4. Heat 1/3 of the oil in a large frying pan over medium heat. Drop 1/4 cup of the fritter mixture into a pan and cook, in batches, for 5 minutes each side or until cooked through
5. Meanwhile, poach remaining 4 eggs in a pan of simmering water for 4-5 minutes or until cooked to your liking
6. Place zucchini fritters on plate, top with mushrooms, poached egg and cherry tomatoes to serve

Much **BETTER BREAKFAST**

WAFFLES WITH SAUTEED *Mushrooms* & MAPLE BACON

Prep: 10 mins   **Cook:** 15 mins   **Serves:** 4

Ingredients

8 (200g) rashers streaky bacon	80g butter, melted
¼ cup maple syrup	1 cup (140g) self-raising flour
1 egg, separated	400g Swiss Brown Mushrooms, halved
1 tbsp caster sugar	2 tbsp chives, sliced
¾ cup (175ml) milk	Sour cream and chives to serve

Method

1. Preheat oven to 180°C fan-forced. Line a baking tray with baking paper
2. Place bacon in a single layer and brush with maple syrup. Cook for 20 minutes or until crisp
3. Place egg yolk, milk, 60g melted butter and flour together in a medium bowl and whisk to combine. Whisk egg whites and sugar in a small bowl until light and fluffy and gently fold into flour mixture
4. Preheat a waffle iron. Use 1/4 cup of the waffle batter at a time. Cook for 4 minutes or until golden
5. Melt remaining butter in a large frying pan over medium high heat. Add mushrooms and chives. Season with salt and pepper. Cook, stirring occasionally for about 5 minutes or until mushrooms are lightly golden
6. Place waffles on serving plates. Top with maple bacon, mushrooms, sour cream and chives

Much EASIER ENTERTAINING

Mushroom Lamb & Feta Gozleme

Prep: 25-40 mins   **Cook:** 6 mins   **Serves:** 4

Ingredients

- 1 tsp caster sugar
- ½ cup (125ml) warm water
- 2 tsp dried yeast
- 3 cups (420g) plain flour
- ½ tsp salt
- ½ cup (125ml) warm milk
- 2 tbsp olive oil
- 1 brown onion, thinly sliced
- 1 garlic clove, crushed
- 400g lamb mince
- 1 tsp ground cumin
- 1 tsp dried oregano
- ½ cup (20g) flat leaf parsley, chopped
- ½ cup (20g) mint leaves, chopped
- 200g Button Mushrooms, sliced
- 200g feta, crumbled
- Lemon wedges, to serve

Method

1. Combine sugar, water and yeast in a jug. Stand for 10 minutes
2. Place flour and salt in a large bowl. Add yeast mixture and milk and combine to make a soft dough. Turn onto a lightly floured board and knead gently until smooth. Divide dough into four portions. Place on a lightly floured board, cover with plastic and stand in a warm place for 20 minutes or until dough has doubled in size
3. Meanwhile, heat half of the oil in a large non-stick frying pan over medium heat. Add onion and garlic and cook, stirring often for 5 minutes or until onion is soft
4. Increase the heat to high, add mince, cumin and oregano and cook, stirring to break up the lumps, for 10 minutes until browned. Transfer to a bowl. Cool for 5 minutes, add parsley and mint
5. Heat remaining oil in same frying pan. Add the mushrooms and cook a further 5 minutes or until browned lightly. Remove from heat
6. On a lightly floured surface roll dough into a 30cm x 40cm rectangle. Place one-quarter of the mince mixture, mushrooms and feta on one half of each rectangle. Season with salt and pepper. Fold dough over to enclose filling. Press edges together to seal
7. Preheat a barbecue plate or frying pan on medium until hot
8. Brush both sides of dough with oil and cook for about 3 minutes or until golden, then turn and cook for a further 3 minutes. Serve with lemon wedges

MEDITERRANEAN Mushroom & CHORIZO SKEWERS

Cook: 8 mins   Serves: 4

Ingredients

- 3 tbs extra virgin olive oil
- 1 lemon, juiced
- 2 tsp smoked paprika
- 2 tsp brown sugar
- 24 button mushrooms
- 3 chorizo sausages (see tip)
- 1 red capsicum
- 1 yellow capsicum
- Tossed salad & lemon wedges, to serve

Method

1. Combine oil, lemon juice, paprika and sugar in a large bowl, season with salt and pepper and whisk until well combined. Add the mushrooms and stir to coat all the mushrooms. Cover and refrigerate for 1 hour to marinate
2. Cut each chorizo into 8 slices. Cut capsicums into pieces. Thread the chorizo, capsicum and mushrooms alternately onto 8 skewers
3. Heat a lightly greased barbecue plate on medium-high. Barbecue the skewers, turning often, for 6-8 minutes or until mushrooms and chorizo are warmed through. Serve with salad and lemon wedges

TIPS & HINTS:

Chorizo is a cured Spanish sausage made from pork and various spices. It has a strong flavour and a firm texture. Chorizo can be eaten raw but taste better cooked.

Much **EASIER ENTERTAINING**

YUMMY BBQ'D MUSHIE

49

THE "ULTIMATE" BEEF & *Mushroom* BURGER

Prep: 10 mins   Cook: 15 mins   Serves: 4

Ingredients

350g beef mince

150g Button Mushrooms, chopped

2 tbsp chopped tarragon

2 tsp Dijon mustard

1 egg, lightly whisked

100g aged cheddar cheese, sliced

4 (100g) rindless bacon rashers

4 Portabella Mushrooms

4 (80g) burger rolls

4 iceberg lettuce leaves, torn

2 vine ripened tomatoes, sliced

¼ cup whole egg mayonnaise

¼ cup tomato chutney

Method

1. Place mince, mushrooms, tarragon, mustard and egg in the bowl of a food processor and blend until combined. Remove from the bowl, season with salt and pepper and form into 4 patties
2. Pre-heat an oiled char-grill pan or BBQ over medium high heat. Cook burger patty for 3-4 minutes, turn and top with sliced cheese. Cook for a further 3-4 minutes or until cheese is melted and patty is cooked to your liking. Set aside to keep warm
3. Cook bacon for 2-3 minutes each side or until golden and crisp, set aside to keep warm
4. Add mushrooms to pan or BBQ, turning until mushrooms are grilled on both sides and warmed through. Remove from the heat
5. Spread base of mushrooms with mayonnaise, top with iceberg lettuce, tomato, beef patty, bacon and drizzle with tomato chutney to serve

PORTABELLA *Mushroom* FRIES

Prep: 15 mins   Cook: 10 mins   Serves: 4-6

Ingredients

FRIES

Vegetable oil, for deep-frying

100g (⅔ cup) plain flour

3 eggs, lighly beaten

2 cups panko breadcrumbs

250g Portabella Mushrooms, stalks trimmed, cut into thin fries

Salt and pepper, to season

HARISSA YOGHURT

2 tsp harissa

1 cup Greek-style yoghurt

Method

FRIES

1. Heat enough oil in a large saucepan to come one-third up the sides to 170°C
2. Meanwhile, place the flour, eggs and breadcrumbs into 3 separate wide, shallow bowls
3. Season the flour well with salt and pepper. Dust the mushroom fries in the flour, shaking off any excess, dip into the egg, then coat well in the breadcrumbs
4. In batches, deep-fry the fries for 5 minutes or until golden and cooked. Drain well on paper towel and season with salt

HARISSA YOGHURT

1. Mix harissa together with yoghurt. Serve with fries

Mushroom & Leek Filo Pie

Prep: 10 mins   Cook: 25 mins   Serves: 4

Ingredients

- 20g butter, plus 50g butter, melted
- 2 leeks, trimmed and sliced
- 300g Button Mushrooms, quartered
- 1 garlic clove, crushed
- 100g baby spinach leaves
- 6 eggs, lightly whisked
- ½ cup thickened cream
- ½ cup (50g) grated cheddar cheese
- 50g full fat fresh ricotta cheese, broken into pieces
- 2 tsp finely grated lemon rind, plus lemon wedges to serve
- 6 sheets filo pastry

Method

1. Preheat oven to 200°C fan-forced. Heat 20g butter in a large deep frying pan over high heat. Add the leeks and mushrooms and cook for 3-5 minutes or until browned. Add garlic and cook, stirring for 1 minute. Remove from the heat and stir in spinach leaves, until just wilted. Set aside to cool slightly
2. Whisk eggs and cream in a medium size bowl. Add mushroom mixture, cheese and lemon rind. Season with salt and pepper
3. Lay a 50cm long piece of baking paper on the bench. Top with 1 layer of filo pastry, brush with melted butter, top with another sheet of filo pastry and repeat until all pastry sheets are layered on top of each other
4. Heat an oiled large deep frying pan with oven-proof handle over medium heat. Lift baking paper sheet into frying pan, easing down the edges into the pan. Stir egg and mushroom mixture and pour into pastry case
5. Scrunch the pastry edges over the mushroom mixture. Transfer to the oven and cook for 20-25 minutes or until the egg is set and the pastry is golden
6. Serve with lemon wedges and freshly ground black pepper

TIPS & HINTS:
Always use fresh refrigerated filo pastry, anything from the freezer will be brittle and break easily

Much **MORE DELICIOUS EVERY DAY**

Mushroom VEGGIE BURGERS

Prep: 10 mins   Cook: 10 mins   Serves: 4

Ingredients

- ⅓ cup (50ml) thick Greek-style yoghurt
- 1 tbsp lemon juice
- 1 tbsp finely chopped mint leaves
- 2 garlic cloves, crushed
- 3 tbsp olive oil
- 200g Button Mushrooms, trimmed and halved
- ½ tsp ground cumin
- ½ tsp ground coriander
- 400g can chickpeas, rinsed and drained
- 1 carrot, peeled and coarsely grated
- ¼ cup (10g) parsley leaves
- Plain flour, for dusting
- 4 (80g each) Ciabatta rolls, halved
- 4 canned baby beets, sliced
- 1 Lebanese cucumber, sliced into ribbons
- 4 butter lettuce leaves

Method

1. Combine yoghurt, lemon juice, 1 garlic clove and mint in a small bowl, set aside
2. Heat 1 tablespoon olive oil in a medium frying pan over medium high heat, add mushrooms. Cook for 4 minutes, add remaining garlic, cumin and coriander and cook for a further 1 minute or until mushrooms are fragrant and golden. Allow to cool slightly
3. Place chickpea, carrot, parsley and mushroom mixture in the bowl of a food processor and blend until just combined. Shape into 4 patties, dust in flour
4. Heat remaining oil in a large frying pan. Cook patties for 3-4 minutes each side or until crisp and golden
5. Place base of rolls on serving platter, spread evenly with yoghurt, top with lettuce, mushroom patty, cucumber and top of roll to serve

TIPS & HINTS:
Drizzle with chilli oil for an extra kick!

Much **MORE DELICIOUS EVERY DAY** •

Mushroom & Char Siu Pork Stir Fry

Prep: 10 mins   Cook: 15 mins   Serves: 4

Ingredients

- ⅓ cup char siu sauce
- 2 tsp Chinese five spiced powder
- 2 tbsp soy sauce
- 1 tbsp peanut oil
- 500g pork fillet (tenderloin), thinly sliced
- 400g Button Mushrooms
- ½ cup (125ml) water
- 2 bunches (480g) gailan (Chinese broccoli), trimmed and cut into 5cm lengths
- 2 green onions, thinly sliced on the angle
- 1 tbsp black sesame seeds
- Rice noodles, to serve

Method

1. Cook rice noodles according to packet instructions. Set aside and keep warm
2. Place char siu and five spice powder in a small jug and mix to combine. Spread 2 tablespoons of mixture onto pork. Add soy sauce to remaining mixture, stir to combine
3. Heat oil in large deep frying pan over medium heat. Add pork, and stir-fry for 6-8 minutes, turning until browned all over. Add mushrooms, cook stirring for 2 minutes, until golden. Add remaining marinade and water to pan and bring to a gentle simmer, about 5 minutes. Remove pork and set aside to rest
4. Add gailan to frying pan, cover and cook 2-3 minutes or until tender. Thickly slice pork and serve with mushrooms and gailan and sprinkle with green onion and black sesame. Serve with rice noodles

Much EASIER ENTERTAINING

Much EASIER ENTERTAINING

MAPLE ROASTED Mushroom & CARROT SALAD

Prep: 10 mins **Cook:** 35 mins **Serves:** 4 as a side salad

##

DRESSING

¼ cup (50ml) maple syrup

2 tbsp olive oil

1 ½ tbsp red wine vinegar

½ tsp chilli flakes

2 bunches (375g each) baby (Dutch) carrots, peeled and trimmed, leaving 1.5cm stalk

1 bunch (375g) baby purple carrots, peeled, halved and trimmed, leaving 1.5cm stalk

400g Swiss Brown Mushrooms, trimmed

¼ cup (40g) roughly chopped hazelnuts

¼ cup (10g) mint leaves

TO SERVE

½ cup Greek-style yoghurt

1 - 2 tbsp lemon juice

Method

DRESSING

1. Preheat oven to 200°C fan forced. Combine maple syrup, oil, vinegar and chilli in a small bowl and whisk to combine

2. Place carrots in a large roasting pan, drizzle with 2 tablespoons maple syrup mixture and toss to combine. Roast 10 minutes

3. Add mushrooms and hazelnuts on a baking tray. Drizzle with remaining maple syrup mixture and season with salt and pepper. Roast for 20-25 minutes or until purple carrots are tender

TO SERVE

1. Combine yoghurt and lemon juice in a small bowl. Drizzle yoghurt dressing over carrots and serve with mint leaves

TIPS & HINTS:

Add rocket leaves and goat curd for a substantial salad.

SWEET POTATO
and lentil patties

 PREP 25 MINS  **COOK** 30 MINS   **MAKES** 12

INGREDIENTS

500g Sweet Potato, peeled, cubed

2 tablespoons olive oil

½ cup brown lentils

1 small onion, finely chopped

2 garlic cloves, crushed

1 teaspoon ground cumin

½ teaspoon ground coriander

½ teaspoon turmeric

60g baby spinach, roughly chopped

⅓ cup plain flour

Natural yoghurt and lemon wedges, to serve

METHOD

1. Preheat oven to 220°C/200°C fan-forced. Line an oven tray with baking paper. Place sweet potato on tray and drizzle with half of the oil. Bake for 15-20 minutes, until tender. Mash in a bowl and set aside

2. Cook lentils in a pan of boiling water for 15-20 minutes, until softened. Drain well. Transfer to a large bowl to cool

3. Meanwhile, heat a little of the remaining oil in a large frying pan on medium. Cook onion and garlic for 4-5 minutes until softened. Add spices and cook for 1 minute until fragrant. Add spinach, stirring until just wilted. Transfer to bowl with lentils and sweet potato. Mix well and season to taste. Chill until cold. Form into patties and toss in flour to coat. Place on a baking paper-lined tray

4. Heat remaining oil in frying pan on medium-high. Cook the patties for 2-3 minutes each side until golden. Drain on paper towel. Serve patties with yoghurt and lemon wedges

TIPS & HINTS:

Brown lentils are also labelled as green lentils. They are larger than the French lentils. For a gluten free option, replace plain flour for gluten-free flour.

Tip
Freeze half the muffins in zip-lock bags for easy snacking

SWEET POTATO
spinach and feta muffins

PREP 30 MINS **COOK** 30 MINS **MAKES** 12

INGREDIENTS

1 cup (150g) plain flour

1 cup (160g) wholemeal plain flour

1 teaspoon bi-carb soda

40g baby spinach leaves, steamed, chopped

2 green onions, sliced thinly

100g feta, crumbled

2 eggs, beaten

⅔ cup (190g) plain Greek-style yoghurt

125g can creamed corn

1 cup Sweet Potato puree

50g butter, melted

¼ cup (20g) grated parmesan

METHOD

1. Preheat oven to 200°C/180°C. Lightly grease a 12-hole muffin pan

2. Sift flours and soda together in a large bowl. Stir in spinach, onion and half of the feta. Combine remaining ingredients in a bowl, whisking well to combine

3. Fold through dry mixture until just combined. Spoon into prepared cases and sprinkle with remaining feta. Bake for 25-30 minutes until cooked when tested with a skewer

TIPS & HINTS:

You will need a 550g Sweet Potato to make enough puree for this recipe.

Tip
Great as a lower carb, wheat free option for lunch or dinner

SWEET POTATO *toast toppers*

 **PREP** 15 MINS   **COOK** 15 MINS   **MAKES** 6

INGREDIENTS

SWEET POTATO TOAST TOPPED WITH MASHED AVOCADO, CHICKEN AND AIOLI

6 slices (5mm thick) Sweet Potato, skin on

1 avocado, mashed

¾ cup baby spinach leaves

1 cup shredded BBQ chicken

¼ cup aioli

SWEET POTATO TOAST TOPPED WITH TOMATO MEDLEY AND BALSAMIC GLAZE

6 slices (5mm thick) Sweet Potato, skin on

200g tomato medley, chopped

½ red onion, thinly sliced

Baby basil leaves and balsamic glaze, to serve

METHOD

SWEET POTATO TOAST TOPPED WITH MASHED AVOCADO, CHICKEN AND AIOLI

1. Preheat oven to 200°C/180°C fan-forced. Line an oven tray with baking paper Arrange slices on tray. Spray with oil and season to taste. Bake for 10-15 minutes until golden and tender

2. Spread toasts with avocado. Top with spinach and chicken, Drizzle with aioli. Serve immediately

SWEET POTATO TOAST TOPPED WITH TOMATO MEDLEY AND BALSAMIC GLAZE

1. Preheat oven to 200°C/180°C fan-forced. Line an oven tray with baking paper. Arrange slices on tray. Spray with oil and season to taste. Bake for 10-15 minutes until golden and tender

2. Top toasts with tomatoes and onion. Sprinkle with basil leaves and drizzle with balsamic glaze. Serve immediately

TIPS & HINTS:

You can also cook toasts in a sandwich press (between 2 sheets of baking paper) for about 5 minutes until browned and tender.

67

SWEET POTATO
and broccoli frittata

 **PREP** 20 MINS  **COOK** 50 MINS **SERVES** 6

INGREDIENTS

500g Sweet Potato, peeled, thinly sliced

Olive oil spray

8 eggs

½ cup (125ml) light thickened cream

¾ cup (90g) grated tasty cheese

100g small broccoli florets, blanched

2 tablespoons shredded basil

METHOD

1. Preheat oven to 200°C/180°C. Lightly grease and line base and sides of a 20 x 30cm rectangular slice pan

2. Place sweet potato on a lined oven tray. Spray with oil and bake for 15-20 minutes until tender

3. Beat eggs, cream and half of the cheese together. Layer sweet potato and broccoli over base of pan. Pour over egg mixture. Sprinkle with basil and remaining cheese

4. Bake for 25-30 minutes until golden and set. Stand for 5 minutes before slicing

MUSHROOM AND
ancient grain salad

 **PREP** 10 MINS **COOK** 20 MINS **SERVES** 4-6 AS A SIDE

INGREDIENTS

1 packet superblend (fibre) – freekeh, green and yellow lentils and beans

80ml (⅓ cup) extra virgin olive oil

2 punnets Swiss Brown Mushrooms, cleaned, quartered

2 lemons, zest finely grated, juiced

1 red onion, halved very finely shaved

1 bunch coriander, finely chopped, including the stems

80g pine nuts, toasted

200g feta, optional

Salt and pepper, to season

METHOD

1. Cook the grain blend according to packet instruction, then drain, set aside and cool

2. Meanwhile, heat 1 tbsp oil in a large frying pan over medium-high heat. Cook the mushrooms for 5 minutes or until golden and cooked. Season with salt and pepper. Turn off the heat and allow to cool

3. Meanwhile, combine the lemon zest and juice with the onion in a large bowl. Add the remaining oil, cooled grain blend, mushrooms, coriander and pine nuts and toss to combine. Season well with salt and pepper. If using, top with the feta to serve

TIPS & HINTS:

Look out for different grain and seed blends in the health-food aisle of the supermarket.

CAESAR SALAD
with hot smoked salmon

 **PREP** 10 MINS   **COOK** 30 MINS   **SERVES** 4

INGREDIENTS

SEED CRISPS

½ cup flaxseeds

½ cup pumpkin seeds

½ cup sesame seeds

½ cup tricolour chia seeds

½ cup almond meal

1 lemon, finely grated rind

1 teaspoon sea salt flakes

1 tablespoon honey

¾ cup water

CAESAR SALAD

100g shaved prosciutto

4 eggs

2 baby cos, leaves separated

300g hot smoked salmon, broken into pieces

Shaved parmesan, to serve

Parsley or chervil leaves, to serve

Purchased creamy Caesar dressing, to serve

METHOD

SEED CRISPS

1. To make crisps, preheat oven to 160°C. Line a large baking tray with baking paper. Place seeds, almond meal, lemon rind, salt, honey and water in a bowl and stir until well combined. Turn mixture out onto prepared tray and spread evenly over tray until about 5mm thick. Bake for 40 minutes. Carefully turn and bake for a further 10 minutes or until dry and crisp. Transfer to a wire rack and cool. When cooled, break into pieces. Store in an airtight container for up to 2 weeks

CAESAR SALAD

1. Increase oven temperature to 200°C. Line a baking tray with baking paper. Place slices of prosciutto onto prepared tray and bake for 10 minutes or until crisp. Transfer to a wire rack and to cool. Break into pieces

2. Bring a saucepan of water to the boil. Add the eggs and simmer for 7 minutes for soft-boiled. Drain and rinse under cold water. Crack eggs and place in a bowl of cold water before peeling (this helps to loosen the shell). Peel shells from eggs and cut into halves

3. Arrange lettuce leaves, salmon, prosciutto and seed crisps onto a large platter. Half eggs and add to salad. Sprinkle with shaved parmesan and parsley or chervil leaves. Serve with the salad dressing

TIPS & HINTS:

Any leftover seed crisps are great to eat as a healthy snack or add them to your next cheeseboard instead of crackers

TUNA AND PESTO
pasta salad

 **PREP** 20 MINS   **COOK** 20 MINS   **SERVES** 4

INGREDIENTS

375g packet high-fibre penne pasta

½ cup basil pesto

1 lemon, juiced

425g can tuna-in-oil, drained and flaked

1 small red onion, finely sliced

2 Lebanese cucumbers, halved lengthways and sliced

250g cherry tomatoes, halved

100g feta cheese, crumbled

½ cup pitted Kalamata olives, halved lengthways

¼ cup fresh basil leaves

METHOD

1. Cook penne pasta in a large saucepan of boiling salted water following packet directions. Drain. Rinse under cold water. Drain in a colander until dry. Transfer to a large bowl

2. Combine pesto and lemon juice in a screw-top jar. Season with salt and pepper. Shake well to combine

3. Add tuna, onion, cucumbers, tomatoes, feta and olives to pasta. Season with pepper. Drizzle with pesto mixture. Gently toss to combine. Scatter with basil leaves

TIPS & HINTS:

We used Vetta High Fibre Penne in this recipe.

LEMON AND HERB
mushroom salad

 PREP 10 MINS SERVES 4

INGREDIENTS

DRESSING

125ml (¼ cup) extra virgin olive oil

Juice of one lemon

2 red chillies, de-seeded and finely chopped

SALAD

250g Button Mushrooms, sliced

4 mini cucumbers

1 bunch flat-leaf parsley, roughly chopped

Salt and pepper, to season

METHOD

DRESSING

1. In a screw-top jar combine olive oil, lemon juice, chillies and a pinch of salt. Put on the lid and shake until well combined

SALAD

1. Add all salad ingredients to a bowl, top with dressing and gently mix to combine. Serve as a side salad with chicken, fish or grilled meat

 PACKED WITH FLAVOUR, THIS DISH MAKES THE PERFECT SIDE SALAD TO ACCOMPANY CHICKEN, FISH OR GRILLED MEAT

Top Tip
Experiment with any fresh herbs of your choice.

GREEN *shakshuka*

PREP 15 MINS   **COOK** 15 MINS   **SERVES** 4

INGREDIENTS

2 tablespoons olive oil

2 leeks, white part only, thinly sliced

1 large green capsicum, deseeded, diced

2 teaspoons ground cumin

1 teaspoon ground coriander

½ teaspoon dried chilli flakes

1 head of broccoli, cut into small florets

4 green onions, thinly sliced

80g baby spinach

1 cup vegetable or chicken stock

½ cup coriander sprigs, roughly chopped

½ cup mint leaves, roughly chopped

4 eggs

1 cup thick Greek yoghurt

1 tablespoon harissa

Extra mint and coriander leaves, to serve

Chargrilled sourdough bread, to serve

METHOD

1. Heat oil in a large heavy-based frying pan over medium heat. Add leek and capsicum and stir until combined. Cook for 5 minutes or until softened. Stir in cumin, coriander and chilli flakes and cook for 1 minute. Add broccoli, green onion, spinach and stock. Stir until combined. Cover and cook for 2 minutes or until vegetables are just tender. Add chopped coriander and mint. Season with salt and pepper

2. Use a spoon to form indentations in the veggie mixture. Crack an egg into each indent. Cover and cook for 5 minutes or until egg whites are just cooked and the yolk is still wobbly. (It will continue to cook on standing.)

3. Meanwhile, place yoghurt into a bowl. Add harissa, salt and pepper. Swirl harissa through yoghurt. Serve shakshuka immediately, topped with harissa yoghurt and extra herbs with bread on the side

ZOODLE AND *mushroom salad*

PREP 15 MINS **COOK** 10 MINS **SERVES** 4

INGREDIENTS

80ml (⅓ cup) extra virgin olive oil

2 tbsp white wine vinegar

Salt and pepper, to season

1 tsp raw sugar

4 zucchini, trimmed

250g Button Mushrooms, halved

1 punnet cherry tomatoes, halved

1 tbsp drained capers in brine

½ cup Sicilian olives, bruised with a knife, pits removed (optional)

1 cups basil leaves

METHOD

1. Preheat the oven to 220°C. Whisk 2 tbsp of the oil with the vinegar, sugar, salt and pepper in a large bowl, whisking until the sugar dissolves. Using a spiraliser or julienne peeler, cut the zucchini into noodles and add to the bowl, tossing well to combine. Set aside to soften

2. Combine the mushrooms, cherry tomatoes and capers on a large oven tray lined with baking paper. Drizzle with the remaining oil, season with salt and pepper and toss well to combine. Roast in the oven for 15 minutes or until the mushrooms are cooked and the tomato skins have burst

3. Remove from the oven and pour the mixture into the bowl with the zoodles, including any pan juices and toss well to combine. Mix in the olives if using, top with basil and serve

Tip

Fritters will keep for up to 3 days in an airtight container in the fridge.

VEGETABLE FRITTERS
with poached egg

 **PREP** 15 MINS  **COOK** 20 MINS  **SERVES** 4

INGREDIENTS

2 large zucchini, trimmed, sliced

2 cups (about 300g) diced pumpkin

1 carrot, trimmed, sliced

1 cup mint leaves

3 green onions, thinly sliced

½ cup frozen peas, thawed

1 ½ cups panko breadcrumbs

½ cup self-raising flour

150g feta cheese, crumbled

5 eggs

⅓ cup olive oil

METHOD

1. Preheat oven to 180°C. Line a baking tray with baking paper. Place zucchini in a food processor and process until finely chopped. Transfer to a clean kitchen cloth and squeeze, over a bowl or the sink, to remove excess liquid. (This prevents the fritters from being soggy). Place zucchini in a large bowl

2. Add pumpkin, carrot and mint to food processor and process until finely chopped. Add to zucchini with onion, peas, breadcrumbs, flour and feta. Lightly whisk 1 egg in a small bowl and add to vegetable mixture. Season. Stir until combined. Form ⅓ cups of the veggie mixture into fritters and place on a tray

3. Heat half the oil in a non-stick frying pan over medium heat. Cook fritters in batches, adding more if needed, for 3 minutes each side or until golden. Transfer to prepared tray and place in oven to cook for 10 minutes or until cooked through

4. Meanwhile, bring a medium saucepan of water to the boil. Reduce heat to low, and when bubbles subside, use a spoon to stir the water until a whirlpool forms. Break an egg into a small bowl and gently slide into whirlpool. Cook for 3 minutes or until white is cooked. Use a slotted spoon to transfer egg to a plate. Repeat with remaining eggs

MUSHROOM & *halloumi falafel*

 PREP 30 MINS + 30 MINS CHILLING   **COOK** 30 MINS   **MAKES** 20

INGREDIENTS

400g button, cup or flat mushrooms

1 tbs olive oil, plus extra for cooking

1 brown onion, finely chopped

2 garlic cloves, crushed

1 tbs greek seasoning

400g can chickpeas, rinsed, drained

1 bunch flat-leaf parsley leaves, chopped

150g halloumi, grated

1 egg

¾ cup dried breadcrumbs (packaged ones)

2 tbs tahini

¼ cup sesame seeds

1 cup Greek-style yoghurt

Lemon wedges and herbs to serve, optional

METHOD

1. Finely chop the mushrooms by hand or put in a food processor, use pulse button to finely chop. Heat oil in a non-stick frying pan over high heat
2. Add the mushrooms, onion and garlic and cook, stirring often, for 8 minutes or until all moisture has evaporated
3. Stir in the seasoning and cook for 1 minute. Set aside to cool for 10 minutes. Drain any excess moisture and transfer to a bowl. Wipe pan clean
4. Meanwhile, process the chickpeas, parsley, halloumi, egg, breadcrumbs and half the tahini until almost smooth. Add to mushrooms, season and mix well
5. Roll one tablespoonful of mixture into a ball, then roll lightly in sesame seeds. Place on a tray. Repeat to make 30 falafels
6. Cover and refrigerate for 30 minutes if time permits. Mix remaining tahini and yoghurt together. Refrigerate until ready to serve
7. Shallow or deep fry falafel in batches, turning often for 5 minutes until golden. Serve warm or at room temperature with tahini yoghurt, lemon and herbs

TIPS & HINTS:

Falafel is great served as finger food or turn into a meal by shaping ¼ cupfuls of mixture into patties and serving with salad and pita bread.

BARLEY NOURISH BOWL
with soft-boiled egg

 PREP 10 MINS   **COOK** 30 MINS   **SERVES** 4

INGREDIENTS

BOWL

450g sweet potato, peeled, diced

1 red onion, cut into thin wedges

Olive oil cooking spray

1 tablespoon Moroccan seasoning

400g can chickpeas, drained

8 green kale leaves, stalk removed

1 cup pearl barley

4 eggs

100g feta cheese, crumbled

¼ cup pepitas

DRESSING

⅓ cup extra virgin olive oil

¼ cup lime juice

1 tablespoon maple syrup

1 teaspoon mild English mustard

METHOD

BOWL

1. Preheat oven to 180°C. Line 3 baking trays with baking paper. Place sweet potato and onion onto a baking tray. Spray with olive oil and season the sweet potato with half the Moroccan seasoning and salt and pepper. Bake for 20 minutes or until softened. Spread chickpeas on another tray. Spray with olive oil and season with remaining Moroccan seasoning, salt and pepper. Roast for 15 minutes or until golden and crisp. Tear kale leaves into 3cm pieces and place into a bowl. Add oil and massage into kale to soften. Place kale onto remaining baking tray and bake for 10 minutes or until crisp

2. Meanwhile, place barley and 3 cups water into a medium saucepan over high heat. Bring to the boil, reduce heat and simmer for 25 minutes or until tender. Drain and cool. Stir through parsley

3. Bring a saucepan of water to the boil. Add the eggs and simmer for 7 minutes for soft-boiled. Drain and rinse under cold water. Crack eggs and place in a bowl of cold water before peeling (this helps to loosen the shell). Peel shells from eggs and cut into halves

DRESSING

1. Whisk oil, lime juice, maple syrup and mustard in a jug. Season with salt and pepper. Add a little dressing to barley and stir until combined. Spoon barley into shallow bowls. Top with chickpeas, sweet potato, onion, kale, feta and egg. Serve sprinkled with pepitas and drizzled with the dressing

Tip
Add shredded chicken for a protein boost

CREAMY TOMATO
and herb fettuccine

PREP 10 MINS **COOK** 25 MINS **SERVES** 4

INGREDIENTS

500g packet high-fibre fettuccine

1 tablespoon olive oil

1 onion, fine diced

2 cloves garlic, crushed

250g tomato passata

1 punnet cherry tomatoes

1 tablespoons basil, chopped

1 tablespoon thyme, chopped

1 tablespoon Worcestershire sauce

½ teaspoon paprika

300ml lite cooking cream

⅓ cup finely grated parmesan

Thyme and basil extra, for serving

METHOD

1. Cook fettuccine pasta according to packet instructions. Drain and set aside. Keep warm
2. Meanwhile, heat olive oil in a large fry-pan over medium heat. Fry onions until soft. Add garlic and cook for 1 more minute
3. Add passata, tomatoes, basil, thyme, Worcestershire sauce and paprika. Stir, bring to the boil, then reduce to a simmer for 20 minutes
4. Remove from heat, and while still hot stir through cream and half the parmesan. Add the warm pasta to the sauce, toss to coat
5. Serve pasta topped with remaining parmesan and fresh herbs

TIPS & HINTS:

We used Vetta High Fibre Fettuccine in this recipe.

CHARGRILLED HERB CHICKEN WITH
freekeh and peach salad

 PREP 15 MINS   **COOK** 25 MINS   **SERVES** 4

INGREDIENTS

8 Lilydale Free Range Chicken Thigh Fillets, fat trimmed, halved

1 cup (185gm) freekeh

2 tblsp parsley leaves, finely chopped + extra leaves, to serve

2 tblsp chives, finely chopped

2 tblsp mint, finely chopped

4 tblsp olive oil

1 small avocado, chopped

2 peaches, cut into wedges

250gm tomato medley, halved

1 bunch watercress, leaves picked

80gm goat's cheese, crumbled

2 tblsp pistachios, toasted, roughly chopped

1 tblsp balsamic vinegar

METHOD

1. Cook freekeh according to packet directions. Rinse under cold water and drain

2. Meanwhile, preheat a barbecue or chargrill pan over medium-high heat. In a small bowl, combine herbs and 2 tblsp olive oil. Season with salt and pepper

3. Place chicken thighs in a large snap lock bag or shallow glass dish and cover with herb oil. Rub to coat

4. Cook chicken for 3 to 4 minutes each side, or until browned and cooked through. Set chicken aside on a plate covered with foil to rest

5. In a large bowl, combine freekeh, avocado, peaches, tomatoes and watercress. Sprinkle with goat's cheese, pistachios and parsley leaves. Drizzle with remaining oil and balsamic vinegar. Season. Serve freekeh salad with chicken

TIPS & HINTS:

You can replace peaches with nectarines.

QUICK & CONVENIENT

SESAME CHICKEN
and brown rice salad bowl

 PREP 10 MINS   **COOK** 15 MINS   **SERVES** 4

INGREDIENTS

1 Free Range Chicken Breast Fillets (approx. 900g), cut in half horizontally

1 tblsp olive oil

2 tblsp sesame seeds

2 tblsp tahini

Juice and zest of 1 lemon

3 cups cooked brown rice

¼ bunch kale, finely shredded

1 cucumber, cut into ribbons

1 avocado, thinly sliced

1 cup sprouts of choice

¼ cup pickled ginger

¼ cup almonds

METHOD

1. Preheat a large non-stick frying pan on medium heat
2. Spread sesame seeds on a large plate and coat chicken with seeds. Season with salt and pepper. Heat oil in frying pan and cook chicken for 3 to 4 minutes each side, or until cooked through
3. Set chicken aside on a plate covered in foil to rest for 5 minutes. Thinly slice chicken
4. To make dressing, combine tahini, zest and juice and 1/4 cup water in a small bowl until smooth and viscous. Season with salt and pepper
5. In a large bowl, combine the rice, kale, cucumber, avocado, and sprouts. Top the salad with the chicken, pickled ginger and almonds. Drizzle dressing before serving

CREAMY AVOCADO PASTA SALAD
with crispy prosciutto

 PREP 10 MINS   **COOK** 15 MINS   **SERVES** 4

INGREDIENTS

DRESSING

- 1 large ripe avocado, halved, seeded and peeled
- ½ cup lime juice
- 1 clove garlic
- ½ cup olive oil
- ½ cup grated parmesan
- ½ cup parsley leaves

PASTA SALAD

- 500g packet high fibre large fussili
- 100g snow peas, thinly sliced
- 30g baby rocket
- 100g packet prosciutto, cooked, and roughly chopped
- 2 tablespoons pine nuts, toasted

METHOD

DRESSING

1. Add all dressing ingredients into a blender or food processor and puree until smooth. Season with sea salt and freshly cracked pepper

PASTA SALAD

1. Cook pasta according to directions, drain and set aside to cool
2. Pour the dressing on top of cooled pasta and gently toss to coat. Add the rocket and snow peas into pasta and gently stir through
3. Place into a serving bowl and sprinkle with prosciutto and pine nuts

TIPS & HINTS:

We used Vetta High Fibre Large Spirals in this recipe.

THAI BASIL
and chicken fried rice

 **PREP** 15 MINS **COOK** 20 MINS **SERVES** 4

INGREDIENTS

2 tblsp peanut oil

1 large red onion, sliced into thin wedges

2 cloves garlic, crushed

1 tblsp finely grated ginger

1 long red chilli, seeded, finely sliced

1 tblsp brown sugar

500gm Lilydale Free Range Chicken mince

1 red capsicum, thinly sliced

175gm green beans, cut into 3cm lengths

4 cups cooked and cooled jasmine rice (1 ⅓ cups (265gm) uncooked rice)

¼ cup sweet chilli sauce

2 tblsp fish sauce

2 tblsp soy sauce

Juice of 1 lime, + extra wedges, to serve

Thai basil leaves and coriander leaves, to serve

METHOD

1. Heat the oil in a wok over medium-high heat. Stir fry the onion for 2-3 minutes until softened. Add the garlic, ginger, chilli and sugar, and cook for a further minute until fragrant

2. Add the chicken mince and cook, breaking up lumps with a wooden spoon, for 10 minutes or until browned

3. Add the capsicum and beans and stir-fry for 2 minutes until vegetables are just tender

4. Add the cooked rice, sweet chilli sauce, fish sauce, soy sauce and lime juice, and stir-fry for 3 minutes until heated through

5. Serve the rice topped with Thai basil, coriander and lime wedges

ONE-PAN
penne bolognese

 PREP 5 MINS **COOK** 30 MINS  **SERVES** 4

INGREDIENTS

1-2 tablespoons olive oil
1 onion, diced
2 garlic, crushed
2 tablespoons tomato paste
500g beef mince
700g passata
1-2 teaspoons dried Italian herbs
3 cups beef stock
1 packet high-fibre penne pasta
200g fresh ricotta
1 cup shredded cheese mix (see tips)
Fresh basil leaves, to serve

METHOD

1. Heat oil in a wide casserole or fry pan over a medium heat. Fry onion and garlic until soft. Stir in tomato paste and cook for a further minute
2. Add beef mince and cook, breaking up with a wooden spoon. Once browned, drain off fat
3. Add passata, stock and dried herbs. Bring to the boil, add penne and stir into sauce. Reduce heat to a simmer, then cover and cook for 20 minutes, or until pasta is al dente. Stir occasionally adding ½ cup water if mix becomes dry
4. Removed from heat. Dollop ricotta on top of pasta, sprinkle over cheese blend and grill for 5-10 minutes or until golden. Finish with fresh basil

TIPS & HINTS:
We used Vetta High Fibre Penne in this recipe.

LEMONGRASS AND CHILLI TENDERLOINS
with cucumber salad

PREP 15 MINS + 30 MINS FOR MARINATING   **COOK** 10 MINS   **SERVES** 4

INGREDIENTS

DRESSING

- 2 tablespoons rice vinegar
- 2 tablespoons coconut sugar
- 1 tablespoon freshly squeezed lime juice
- 1 tablespoon fish sauce

TENDERLOINS

- 500g Free Range Chicken Tenderloins
- 1 stalk lemongrass, roughly chopped
- 2 shallots
- 2 small red chillies, stalks trimmed
- 2 cloves garlic
- 1 tablespoon grated ginger
- 1 coriander plant, including the root, rinsed well
- ½ cup coconut cream
- 2 teaspoons fish sauce
- 1 tablespoon coconut sugar
- Lime, fresh coriander leaves and sliced red chilli, to serve
- ½ cup salted peanuts, to serve

SALAD

- 2 Lebanese cucumbers, shaved lengthways with a vegetable peeler
- ½ small red onion, cut into fine wedges
- ¼ cup coriander leaves

METHOD

DRESSING

1. To make the dressing, combine the rice vinegar, coconut sugar, lime juice and fish sauce in a jug

TENDERLOINS

1. Combine the lemongrass, shallots, 2 red chillies, garlic, ginger, coriander, coconut cream, fish sauce and coconut sugar in a small food processor and process to form a paste
2. Thread the chicken tenderloins onto skewers and pour over just enough marinade to coat the chicken (remaining marinade can be stored in the refrigerator for up to 1 week).
3. Marinate the chicken in the refrigerator for 30 minutes
4. Chargrill the tenderloins over a medium heat for 2-3 minutes on each side or until cooked through
5. Garnish with lime, coriander, sliced red chilli and peanuts. Pour over the dressing just before serving

SALAD

1. Place the cucumber, red onion and coriander leaves in a serving plate alongside the chargrilled tenderloins.

Tip

Eggs are an excellent source of protein

SPICY SCRAMBLED *egg breakfast rolls*

 PREP 10 MINS   **COOK** 6-8 MINS   **SERVES** 4

INGREDIENTS

4 x 15cm pieces French bread stick (or use 4 long bread rolls)

¼ cup peri peri spicy mayonnaise

6 large eggs, at room temperature

⅓ cup milk

½ tsp dried chilli flakes

2 tbs butter, chopped

60g rocket leaves

METHOD

1. Halve bread and spread cut sides with mayonnaise
2. Use a fork to whisk eggs, milk and chilli flakes in a bowl until just combined. Set aside for a few minutes to allow foam to settle
3. Heat a medium non-stick frying pan over medium heat. Add butter, melt and swirl to coat pan base. Add egg mixture and cook without stirring for 30 seconds
4. Using a wide spatula, push the set eggs around outer edge toward the centre of the pan, tilting the pan to allow the uncooked egg to run over the base. Gently push eggs around pan every 15 seconds until soft folds form and one quarter mixture is unset. Remove from heat
5. Gently fold the egg mixture once more. Divide scrambled eggs and rocket between bread. Season and serve

Tip

This is a great dish for using up those leftover veggies

AUSSIE BUBBLE AND SQUEAK WITH FRIED
egg topper

 PREP 10MINS   **COOK** 15 MINS **SERVES** 2

INGREDIENTS

1 tbs olive oil + cooking oil spray

500g leftover roasted vegetables (such as sweet potato, pumpkin, potato and carrots), roughly chopped

1 cup frozen peas

2 eggs, at room temperature

METHOD

1. Heat oil in a medium non-stick frying pan over medium heat. Add roasted vegetables and cook, tossing often, for 4-5 minutes until vegetables are hot and crisp at the edges. Toss through peas and keep warm over low heat

2. Spray a separate medium non-stick frying pan with oil to grease. Heat over medium heat. Crack eggs into pan and fry until cooked to your liking. Top vegetables with fried eggs, season and serve

tip

This recipe is great for fussy kids as they can't resist the star shaped toast!

SCRAMBLED EGGS WITH
star toast

 PREP 5 MINS   **COOK** 10 MINS   **SERVES** 2

INGREDIENTS

4 eggs, lightly beaten

2 tbsp full cream milk or cream

15g Western Star Spreadable, plus extra for toast

4 thick slices white, brown or multigrain bread

METHOD

1. Place the eggs and milk into a medium bowl and season with salt and pepper. Whisk until frothy

2. Melt Western Star Spreadable in a medium non-stick frying pan over a medium heat. Once melted, add the eggs, and stir gently with a wooden spoon for 2 minutes or until the eggs are just set. Remove the pan from the heat

3. Place the slices of bread in the toaster, and toast until golden. Once toasted, spread with Western Star Spreadable, and then get the kids to help you use a cookie cutter to cut into star shapes

4. Serve the eggs immediately with the star toast

Treats

The perfect blend of salty and sweet

CHOCOLATE POPCORN *cupcakes*

 **PREP** 15 MINS  **COOK** 10 MINS   **SERVES** 12

INGREDIENTS

BASE

½ cup coconut oil, melted

¼ cup coconut sugar

¼ cup desiccated coconut

1 cup hazelnut meal or almond meal

⅓ cup rolled oats

2 tablespoons cacao

FILLING

1 cup nut butter of choice

½ cup coconut oil, melted and slightly cooled

3 tablespoons agave nectar

1 teaspoon vanilla extract

4 cups Sea Salt Popcorn

TOPPING

2 tablespoons coconut oil, melted and cooled

1-2 tablespoons cacao

METHOD

BASE

1. Pre-heat oven to 180°C or 160°C fan forced. Line a standard 12-hole muffin tin with muffin cases

2. Combine base ingredients in a medium bowl and divide evenly between prepared muffin cases. Gently press into cases to flatten

3. Bake for 10 minutes, remove from oven and cool

FILLING

1. Combine all filling ingredients in a medium bowl. Pour over cooled bases pressing in gently to secure

TOPPING

1. Add topping ingredients to a small bowl and whisk to combine

2. Using a spoon, drizzle over the top of the popcorn then place in the fridge for 1 hour or until set

SPICY STRAWBERRY
and jalapeno salsa

PREP 15 MINS   **SERVES** 4

INGREDIENTS

2-3 x 250g punnets strawberries (about 20 strawberries) washed and hulled

½ Spanish onion, finely diced

1 jalapeno, chopped

¼ cup coriander chopped

Juice of 1 lime (about 1 tbsp)

Freshly cracked black pepper

168g packet Cobs By the Sea Salt Naked Corn Chips

METHOD

1. Dice the strawberries into small pieces. Then, combine remaining ingredients in a medium bowl. Toss well

2. Serve immediately with Cobs By the Sea Salt Naked Corn Chips

POPCORN
coconut slice

PREP 5 MINS   **COOK** 5 MINS   **SERVES** 10-12

INGREDIENTS

⅓ cup honey

30g butter

5 Medjool dates, pitted and chopped

120g packet Lightly Salted, Slightly Sweet Popcorn

½ cup pecans, chopped

⅓ cup mixed fruit & nuts (we used Goji Berry Super mix) plus extra for on top

METHOD

1. Grease and line a lamington pan
2. Combine the popcorn, pecans and berry/nut mix in a medium bowl
3. Heat honey, butter and dates in a small saucepan over medium heat, stirring until melted
4. Pour into the popcorn bowl and stir to combine
5. Press into prepared lamington pan, sprinkle with extra berries, nuts and coconut. Chill 30 minutes or until firm. Slice into portions

Tip
This popcorn slice can be whipped up in 10 minutes

PIZZA POPCORN

 PREP 5 MINS   **COOK** 10 MINS **SERVES** 4

INGREDIENTS

80g packet Sea Salt Popcorn

40g butter, softened

1 tablespoon pizza sauce

2 teaspoon Tuscan seasoning

1 teaspoon paprika

1 teaspoon garlic powder

1 teaspoon oregano

METHOD

1. Pre-heat oven to 180°C/160°C fan forced, grease and line 2 oven trays
2. Grease and line 2 oven trays
3. Combine butter, spices and pizza sauce
4. Put popcorn into a large bowl, add the butter and spices. Stir to combine
5. Spread onto the trays evenly in a single layer. Bake for 10 minutes, stirring half way through
6. Remove from oven and pour into a bowl and serve

tip

A twist on the traditional, try with fried egg instead

RAMEN NOODLES
with fried eggs

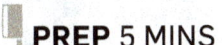 **PREP** 5 MINS   **COOK** 5 MINS   **SERVES** 2

INGREDIENTS

2 x 120g packs ramen noodles
½ cup frozen peas
100g red capsicum, chopped
2 tablespoons soy sauce
1 teaspoon sesame oil
3 green onions, sliced
4 fried eggs

METHOD

1. Cook the ramen noodles according to packet instructions. Two minutes before draining, add the peas and capsicum and continue simmering with the noodles, then drain, reserving one tablespoon cooking liquid and return to the pan

2. To serve, toss the combined soy, sesame oil and cooking liquid through the noodles along with the green onions and divide between bowls. Serve topped with fried eggs and a sprinkle of dried chilli if desired

Tip
keep the carbs low and use fresh zucchini noodles

SUN-DRIED TOMATO, TUNA AND OLIVE
zucchini noodles

 PREP 5 MINS   **COOK** 5 MINS   **SERVES** 2

INGREDIENTS

250g Ricotta Pasta Stir through, Sundried Tomato

2 spring (green) onions, trimmed and thinly sliced

⅓ cup pitted Kalamata olives

500g fresh spiralised zucchini noodles (see note)

185g can tuna in olive oil, drained and roughly flaked

Salt and pepper, to taste

⅓ cup small basil leaves

Perfect Italiano parmesan, finely grated, to serve

METHOD

1. Heat a large non-stick frying pan over medium to low heat. Add Ricotta Pasta Stir-through, Sundried Tomato, spring onions and olives. Gently stir to combine and heat until hot

2. Gently toss through zucchini noodles. Add tuna, season to taste. Sprinkle with basil and parmesan. Serve with a leafy salad if desired

NOTE
Spiralised zucchini noodles are available in the fresh produce section in most large supermarkets. To make 500g spiralised zucchini noodles, you'll need about 600g zucchini. Spiralise the zucchini using a spiraliser or julienne peeler to create long thin ribbons.

Tip

You can use leftover rice in this recipe

FRIED RICE
with eggs

 **PREP** 10 MINS   **COOK** 15 MINS   **SERVES** 4

INGREDIENTS

8 eggs, medium hard boiled

2 tablespoons canola oil

115g punnet baby corn, halved lengthways

100g snow peas, trimmed and halved

1 clove garlic, crushed

2 teaspoons finely grated ginger

2 cups shredded Chinese cabbage

4 cups cooked long grain rice

⅓ cup soy sauce

4 green onions, sliced

½ cup bean sprouts, trimmed

METHOD

1. Heat the oil in a wok or large deep frying pan over medium heat
2. Cook the baby corn for 1-2 minutes then add the snow peas, garlic and ginger. Cook for another 1-2 minutes until tender
3. Toss the cabbage in the wok, cook for a minute until starting to wilt then stir in the rice and cook for 4-5 minutes until heated through
4. Stir the soy through the rice, and cook for another 2-3 minutes, moving the rice around the wok to mix in with the soy evenly
5. To serve, cut the egg into thick slices. Divide the rice between serving bowls and top with egg, a scatter of green onions and bean sprouts

HEALTHIER CHICKEN SCHNITZEL BURGERS
with avocado smash

 PREP 15 MINS   **COOK** 25 MINS   **SERVES** 4

INGREDIENTS

400g Free Range Herb Ciabatta Chicken Schnitzels

½ cup reduced fat Greek-style natural yoghurt

2 tablespoons medium peri peri sauce

4 sourdough or seeded bread rolls, halved

4 small ice-berg lettuce leaves

2 Lebanese cucumbers, thinly sliced lengthways

Sweet potato fries, to serve

Avocado smash

1 large ripe avocado

1 tablespoon lemon juice

75g feta, crumbled

METHOD

1. Cook free range herb ciabatta chicken schnitzels following packet directions.

2. Meanwhile, to make avocado smash, halve avocado lengthways, remove the seed and roughly chop. Place into a bowl. Add lemon juice and season with salt and pepper. Roughly mash with a fork. Stir through feta. Set aside.

3. Combine yoghurt and peri peri sauce in a small bowl until smooth. Set aside.

4. Toast bread rolls. Divide avocado smash between bread rolls. Top roll bases with lettuce and cucumber. Halve schnitzels. Top each burger with a schnitzel. Drizzle with peri peri yoghurt and top with roll tops. Serve with remaining peri peri yoghurt and sweet potato fries.

www.ingramcontent.com/pod-product-compliance
Lightning Source LLC
LaVergne TN
LVHW060159080526
838202LV00052B/4170